THE
INFOGRAPHIC
GUIDE TO
PERSONAL FINANCE

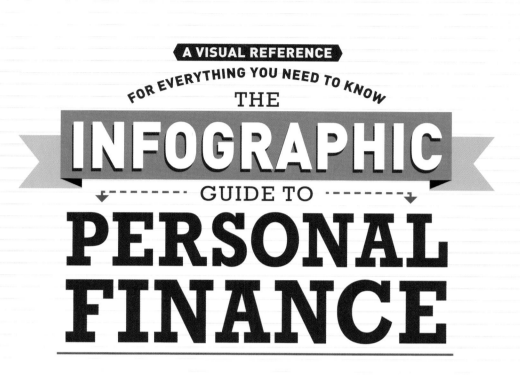

A VISUAL REFERENCE
FOR EVERYTHING YOU NEED TO KNOW

THE
INFOGRAPHIC
GUIDE TO
PERSONAL
FINANCE

MICHELE CAGAN, CPA, and ELISABETH LARIVIERE

Adams Media
New York   London   Toronto   Sydney   New Delhi

Adams Media
An Imprint of Simon & Schuster, Inc.
57 Littlefield Street
Avon, Massachusetts 02322

First Adams Media trade paperback edition DECEMBER 2017

ADAMS MEDIA and colophon are trademarks of Simon and Schuster.

For information about special discounts for bulk purchases, please contact Simon & Schuster Special Sales at 1-866-506-1949 or business@simonandschuster.com.

The Simon & Schuster Speakers Bureau can bring authors to your live event. For more information or to book an event contact the Simon & Schuster Speakers Bureau at 1-866-248-3049 or visit our website at www.simonspeakers.com.

Interior design by Elisabeth Lariviere
Interior design on pages 26, 27, 30, 31, 38, 39, 40, 41, 50, 51, 54, 55, 56, 57, 78, 79, 82, 83, 88, 89, 94, 95 by Heather McKiel
Interior design on pages 96, 97, 120, 121 by Frank Rivera
Interior images © Shutterstock, iStockphoto.com, Getty Images, and 123RF

Manufactured in the United States of America

10 9 8 7 6 5

ISBN 978-1-5072-0466-5
ISBN 978-1-5072-0484-9 (ebook)

Contents

CHAPTER 1

BUDGETING AND SAVING

CHAPTER 2

SPENDING

CHAPTER 3

DEBT AND CREDIT

CHAPTER 4

INVESTING

HOUSING

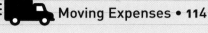

INTRODUCTION

Personal finance is one of the most important life skills to master, yet it's one of the few topics rarely covered in school. Still, the moment you move into adulthood, you're expected to know how to manage your finances successfully, despite the fact that you've never been taught the basics of how to do that. That's what this book is all about: giving you the building blocks of a complete personal finance education so you can take charge of your money and your financial future.

This set of fifty colorful, easy-to-reference infographics offers detailed explanations of the most important personal finance concepts. Whether you're looking to get a better handle on your student loan debt, craft a budget you can really live with, or start building your personal wealth, this handy guide can help you get there. With this book's comprehensive yet concise charts, lists, and graphs, you'll learn everything you need to know, from how to choose the best credit card for you, to the ins and outs of successfully selling your house. Essential concepts are discussed, including banking basics, retirement planning, and establishing credit.

You'll learn the easiest ways to dig out of debt, what to do if you're the victim of identity theft, and how to successfully research and invest in stocks. You'll also find useful tips for boosting your income; using your income tax refund to further your financial goals; shopping for the right car insurance; avoiding hidden costs lurking in your budget; spending less on every grocery bill; deciding whether it makes more sense to rent or buy your next place; and choosing the right financial adviser for you.

From creating your first budget to buying your first house to making your first investment, *The Infographic Guide to Personal Finance* offers wide-ranging financial strategies in a fresh, new format.

CHAPTER 1

BUDGETING AND SAVING

Your Budget
by the Numbers

Creating a livable budget seems confusing, but it's really simple—especially when you start with the big picture.

The best getting-started guideline is the 50-30-20 rule. That standard helps define your big spending buckets, but allows flexibility inside the buckets based on your unique situation.

Big Spending Buckets

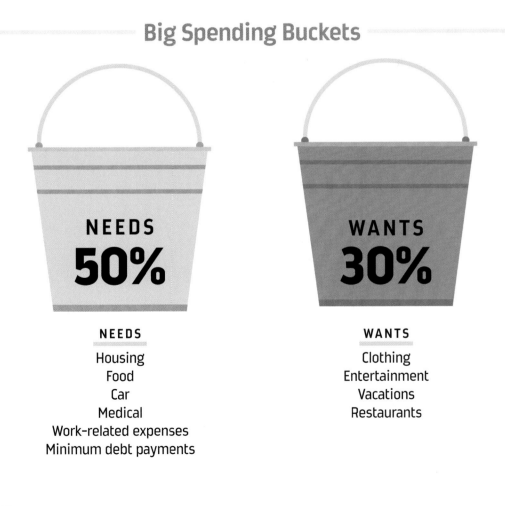

NEEDS
50%

WANTS
30%

NEEDS

Housing
Food
Car
Medical
Work-related expenses
Minimum debt payments

WANTS

Clothing
Entertainment
Vacations
Restaurants

A Closer Look at Needs

Your "Needs" bucket holds everything you absolutely must have to survive—the basics. Not sure how much to budget for housing or transportation? Follow these guideposts (and stay inside the 50% bucket cap).

Housing (including utilities)	**25-35%**
Food (basic groceries)	**5-10%**
Car (including insurance and gas)	**7-10%**
Medical (including health insurance)	**5-10%**
Work-related expenses (including child care)	**5-10%**
Minimum debt payments (credit cards and personal loans)	**2-5%**

SAVINGS & INVESTMENTS

20%

SAVINGS & INVESTMENTS

Emergency fund
Retirement plan
Extra debt payments

—TIP—

Figure out your budget based on take-home pay, not gross pay.

—TIP—

If your "Needs" exceed 50%, steal from your "Wants" bucket.

CALCULATING YOUR NET WORTH

ASSETS:

EVERYTHING YOU OWN

EXAMPLE:

🐷	SAVINGS AND INVESTMENTS	**$14,000**
🏠	HOUSE	**$325,000**
💰	RETIREMENT FUNDS	**$32,000**
🚗	CAR	**$15,000**
	TOTAL ASSETS	**$386,000**

TOTAL ASSETS − TOTAL LIABILITIES

COUNTRIES WITH THE HIGHEST MEDIAN NET WORTH (IN US DOLLARS)

Switzerland	$244,000	New Zealand	$136,000	UK	$108,000
Australia	$163,000	Japan	$120,000		

When it comes to tracking your personal financial health, the best thermometer is your net worth. This simple calculation lets you measure financial progress, so you can see whether you're gaining or losing ground, and keep your finances on track. Smart money strategies—like paying down debt and saving for retirement—send your net worth higher and beef up your financial fitness. Imprudent moves, like shopping sprees and ballooning credit card debt, can put your net worth on life support.

LIABILITIES:

EVERYTHING YOU OWE

EXAMPLE:

MORTGAGE	$256,000
STUDENT LOANS	$33,000
CAR LOAN	$7,500
CREDIT CARD DEBT	$10,000
TOTAL LIABILITIES	**$306,500**

⇒ = NET WORTH $79,500

Italy	$104,000	Canada	$97,000	Germany	$43,000
Singapore	$101,000	Denmark	$52,000	Sweden	$40,000
France	$100,000	US	$45,000		

5 STEPS FOR CREATING
a Budget You Can Stick To

Developing a budget can do more than track your spending and savings. It can also help you work toward your financial goals. The following steps will show you how to build a budget that works for your life, so you don't have to worry about falling short of your plans.

1 START WITH YOUR GOALS

Write down your financial goals. Be sure to include actual dollar amounts and time frames to make tracking possible. For example, measurable goals would be "Have a $1,000 emergency fund by April 1" and "Pay off $5,000 credit card debt in eighteen months." Then divide the dollar amount by the number of months to figure out your monthly goals.

2 KNOW YOUR INCOME

Before you can establish a budget, you have to know exactly how much money you have coming in every month from your employer and other sources. Make sure to include only the money you actually receive (for example, the exact amount of your paycheck rather than your gross pay).

3 TOTAL YOUR MONTHLY EXPENSES

You'll need to know how much money you're spending every month. When figuring out your total monthly expenses, be sure to include groceries, rent or mortgages, all debt payments (including car loans, student loans, and credit cards), cell phone service, cable, and entertainment. Remember to include occasional expenses, like doctor visits and car insurance. Look through bank and credit card statements to get a realistic picture of your spending.

4 CREATE A REALISTIC BUDGET

To make your first stab at a budget, add your monthly expenses from Step 3 to the monthly goals you calculated in Step 1, then subtract that total from your monthly income. If the balance is positive, you've created a budget that is compatible with your current lifestyle. If the balance is negative, take another look at your goals, expenses, and income.

5 REVISIT YOUR GOALS AND EXPENSES

If the first draft of your budget came out negative, rework the numbers and try again. Think about what areas you may be able to alter in order to create a budget that's manageable and still fits your needs. For example, you can revisit your expenses, and decide which are priority items that need to stay in your budget and which you can do without. You can consider changing the amount of time or money needed to meet your goals. Or you can figure out a way to increase your income. Any one of those changes could make your budget come together.

BANKING BASICS

	BANKS	**CREDIT UNIONS**
RATES & FEES	Charge higher fees and loan rates and offer lower savings rates.	Offer higher savings rates and charge lower fees and loan rates.
ACCESS	Typically have more branches and ATMs, and use newer technology.	Have fewer branches and ATMs, but often have branch partners (so you get services at a different credit union and use other ATMs), and are usually slower to embrace new technology.

WHO DO THEY WORK FOR?

Banks are for-profit and try to maximize profits for their stockholders. Credit unions are not-for-profit and work to benefit their members (people who have accounts there)— usually offering much better customer service.

Where you keep money affects your finances more than you realize. Different types of financial institutions serve up different offerings, from loan rates to banking fees. Once you've chosen the spot to stash your cash, you'll still need to figure out the best types of accounts to use. Here's what you need to know.

4 ACCOUNTS AND WHEN TO USE THEM

 CHECKING ACCOUNTS: Unrestricted access, so perfect for everyday spending; usually don't earn interest; most charge monthly maintenance fees.

 SAVINGS ACCOUNTS: Quick but restricted access to the money (six withdrawals per month), so good for small, short-term savings goals; earn interest; no fees.

 MONEY MARKET ACCOUNTS: Quick but restricted access to the money (six withdrawals per month) with high minimum-balance requirements, so good for emergency savings; earn more interest than standard savings accounts; may charge low-balance fees.

 **CERTIFICATES OF DEPOSIT (CDS):** Limited access to the money for a locked-in time period, so good for long-term savings; usually earn the highest interest rates, with higher rates for longer lock-in periods; penalties for early withdrawals.

 **BANK ON THIS**

Savings accounts (including money markets and CDs) are for money you can't afford to lose. Your money is 100% guaranteed safe with guaranteed interest earnings—unlike investments, which are never guaranteed.

The PROS and CONS of JOINT CHECKING ACCOUNTS

PROS

✓ **CONVENIENCE.** Having a joint checking account makes it easier to pay for expenses and bills. Both partners are aware of how much money is available, and they can tackle bills efficiently instead of constantly shuffling money from one account to another.

✓ **EASY TO KEEP TRACK OF BILLS.** With a single checking account, it's easy to see which bills have been paid and which haven't. It also streamlines the process since either partner can pay the bills when they're due.

✓ **TEAMWORK.** Many couples have different incomes, which can sometimes lead to feelings of inequality. By joining finances, both partners are responsible for the same pool of money, rather than acting like separate entities. This creates a team atmosphere and allows partners to share funds equally.

✓ **REDUCES FEES.** Many checking accounts require that you have a minimum balance in order to avoid maintenance fees or overdraft fees. By having one joint account, you can reduce those bank fees since you're both putting money into one account and can reach that minimum balance much more easily.

If you're moving in with a significant other for the first time or just got married, you may be wondering whether you should merge your financial accounts. After all, it may seem easier than dividing up expenses and writing out separate checks for everything. Here's what you should know before you make this important financial decision.

CONS

✗ **POTENTIAL FOR FIGHTS ABOUT MONEY.** Since both of you will share the account, you and your partner may feel like you need to discuss everything you buy and justify your spending. If you're used to being more independent, this may lead to arguments about money.

✗ **HIGHLIGHTS DIFFERENT SPENDING STYLES.** It can be very difficult to make a joint account work if you and your partner have different spending styles. If you like to save and your partner tends to go on shopping sprees, set some spending boundaries. That way, you'll discuss large purchases before making them.

✗ **NO PRIVACY.** Joint accounts mean that all of your transactions are completely transparent. While this can be a good thing in many cases, it also makes it harder to purchase things like gifts for the other person or personal items you may want to keep private.

✗ **DIFFICULT TO SEPARATE.** If you and your partner part ways later on, it can be difficult to separate your account and finances. To make matters worse, each person has equal access to the account, so they have the right to withdraw funds and close the account at any time and without the other person's consent.

HOW YOUR
Money Grows

TIME MATTERS

The longer your money has to compound, the bigger it will grow, which is why it's extra important to start saving for retirement as soon as possible.

LET'S SAY YOU CONTRIBUTE $2,000 A YEAR TO YOUR 401(K) EARNING 6% A YEAR.

If you start saving at age twenty-five, by the time you're sixty-five you'll have $328,101. But if you wait until you're forty-five to start contributing that $2,000 a year, you'll end up with $77,986—less than a quarter of what you'd have if you started at twenty-five.

FREQUENCY MATTERS   INTEREST TYPICALLY COMPOUNDS ANNUALLY, QUARTERLY, OR MONTHLY. THE MORE OFTEN THE COMPOUNDING TAKES PLACE, THE FASTER YOUR MONEY WILL GROW.

WHAT IS COMPOUNDING?

Compounding is one very important way that your money grows, and it's the main reason that starting to save as soon as possible—in your 20s and 30s—is crucial for building wealth. Compounding lets you earn money on your investment earnings: interest, dividends, and capital gains (stock price growth). For example, you have an initial investment in a money market account and it earns interest. That interest gets added to your original investment. Now you'll be earning interest on your interest. And over a long period of time, you'll see your investment grow to truly astounding heights.

STARTING AT . . . . BY AGE 45 . . . . BY AGE 65

25   **$77,986**   **$328,101**

STARTING AT . . . . BY AGE 45 . . . . BY AGE 65

35   **$27,943**   **$167,606**

STARTING AT . . . . BY AGE 65

45   **$77,986**

THE RULE OF 72

The Rule of 72 lets you figure out how soon your investment will double using a specific interest rate (or rate of return for non-interest earnings on investments, like growth and dividends). Simply divide the interest rate into 72. The answer tells you how many years it will take your money to double. So if your money is earning 5% a year, the calculation would be 72 ÷ 5 = 14.4. Your money would double in a little over fourteen years based on compounding alone.

5 WAYS TO BOOST YOUR INCOME THIS MONTH

1

GET A SECOND JOB

Finding a second job can be an effective way to increase your household's income.

2

FREELANCE

You can sign up on websites like *Upwork* and *Freelancer* to build a profile and find detailed opportunities that fit your skills.

3

DRIVE AROUND TOWN

Check out popular services like Uber or Lyft to find out how you can boost your income on a regular basis.

If you've reduced your expenses as much as you can and still have trouble finding the money to reach your financial goals, consider temporarily or permanently adding to your income. The following options can help you make enough money to pay off debts or significantly increase your savings. However, keep in mind that you may need to make some short-term sacrifices, such as spending less time hanging out with friends and family, in order to make the most of these opportunities.

4

JOIN A DIRECT SALES COMPANY

While a direct sales company can be a great way to bring in a second income and gain entrepreneurial skills, keep in mind that joining these companies often requires up-front fees and the purchase of inventory.

5

RENT OUT YOUR HOME

If you own a spacious home, you may want to consider renting out extra bedrooms or a finished basement on websites like *Airbnb*, *Zillow*, or *Craigslist*.

EMERGENCY FUNDS
CAN SAVE THE DAY

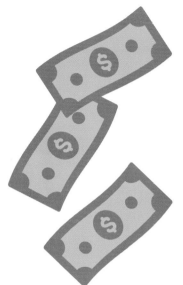

Cars break down, pipes burst, jobs disappear. Emergency expenses crop up randomly. You can't predict them, but you can plan for them with an emergency fund. To cover virtually any financial jam, stash enough money to cover three to six months' worth of living expenses in your emergency account. It can take a while to save that much, so start right away and you'll be ready for that inevitable rainy day.

THE BEST EMERGENCY FUND WILL HAVE THESE KEY FEATURES:

+ **Separate from your everyday accounts**

+ **No (or very low) transaction fees**

+ **Easy access**

+ **No penalties for withdrawals**

+ **Interest earnings on the balance**

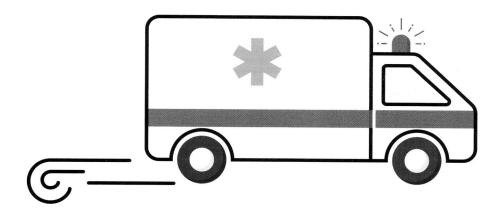

Without an emergency fund, you'll be scrambling when an unexpected expensive crisis crops up. Check out what happens to Americans who don't have emergency savings to fall back on:

13% have to borrow from their retirement accounts

10% take hardship withdrawals from their retirement savings

16% are late with their mortgage payments

19% overdraw their checking accounts

21% struggle with overdue medical bills

15% can't afford to get a prescription filled

6 USES FOR YOUR TAX REFUND
TO MOVE YOUR FINANCES FORWARD

While you may be tempted to spend your tax refund on an extravagant vacation or the latest thing in tech, you can also use it to improve your finances. Depending on your current financial situation and goals, you may want to consider these alternatives to help you boost your finances.

1

Put It Toward Your Retirement

You should consider using your tax refund to beef up your retirement accounts, especially if you haven't been saving as much as you'd like.

2

Pay Off Credit Card Debt

If you have a lot of credit card debt (which usually comes with high interest charges), consider using your tax refund to pay down that debt. Putting your tax refund toward your credit card balance will help you dig out of debt and gain financial freedom much quicker.

3

Add to Your Emergency Fund

By putting your tax refund into your emergency fund, you can have peace of mind knowing that you have the money needed to cover things that may come up throughout the year, such as a flat tire or a medical procedure.

4

Save for Future Big-Ticket Purchases

It can be hard to save for a future big-ticket purchase, such as a car or a new home, so putting away your tax refund for this expense can help you get to your goal faster.

5

Buy Stocks

If you've been thinking about putting some money into the stock market, now may be the time to consider investing. You can use your tax refund to open a brokerage account and start buying corporate shares or exchange-traded funds (ETFs), which are similar to mutual funds when it comes to diversification, but are much easier to trade.

6

Invest in Yourself

One way to boost your future finances is to increase your value in the working world. Consider using your tax refund to further your education or take courses that strengthen your job skills and prepare you for the position you wish you had.

WHEN TO REEVALUATE YOUR BUDGET

GET A RAISE

Figure out the best way to use that extra cash: whether that's paying down debt, spending it, or saving it.

BUY A HOUSE

Adjust your budget to include your mortgage payments and a bigger contribution to an emergency fund to cover unexpected household expenses.

GET MARRIED OR MOVE IN TOGETHER

Combining two households into one can bring more breathing room to your budget.

HAVE A BABY

Adding a family member calls for long-term changes in your budget. Keep unnecessary expenses to a minimum and start saving for college.

Your budget needs to adapt and evolve to fit your life under changing circumstances. As your income, expenses, goals, and lifestyle change over time, rework your budget to fit your new financial reality.

RECOVER FROM A FINANCIAL EMERGENCY

Retool your budget to replenish your emergency fund, so you'll be prepared for whatever comes next.

MOVE TO A NEW CITY

Revamp your budget to account for your new cost of living.

PAY OFF DEBT

Without that student loan or credit card payment draining your budget, you can add back some of the expenses you've cut, or budget that extra money into long-term savings.

LOSE A JOB

This temporary situation calls for an immediate budget makeover. Slash spending and increase income in any way you can.

10 Ways to
PROTECT YOUR FINANCIAL INFO

With identity theft, data breaches, ransomware, and spyware becoming disturbingly commonplace, it's more important than ever to safeguard your financial information, especially if you conduct most of your financial business online.

Take these ten steps to protect your accounts, information, and financial well-being.

Secure your hardware. Keep the security protocols up to date, make sure your security software is never turned off, log out of your accounts when finished, and password-protect your devices.

Beware of public settings. Never use unsecured Wi-Fi connections for anything that requires a password, and keep your RFID-enabled cards (the kind you wave to pay with) in an RFID-blocking wallet. (RFID stands for radio-frequency identification.)

Change your passwords. Reset your financial log-in passwords every ninety days, and don't use the same password for more than one account.

Secure your apps. Turn on the security settings for all apps related to your finances, and choose the highest security setting available.

 Encrypt your data. Use a secure browser, and always look for the data encryption "lock" icon in the status bar before entering a password.

 Limit social sharing. Don't give criminals the answers to financial challenge questions, like your pet's name, your mother's maiden name, or your favorite band.

 Protect your papers. Keep your financial documents in a secure location, and shred everything you no longer need before you get rid of it.

 Check your credit. Look carefully for any activity that isn't yours.

 Secure your credit. If you think you're vulnerable to identity theft, place a fraud alert or security freeze on your credit reports.

 Read your statements. Review your credit card statements (and other accounts) every month and report any unfamiliar charges or claims.

CHAPTER 2
SPENDING

BETTER SPENDING HABITS

DON'Ts

 Buy brand-name products.

 Use an out-of-network ATM. Most banks charge "foreign" ATM fees every time you use an out-of-network ATM, and those fees can really add up.

 Buy lottery tickets.

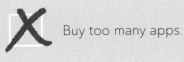 Buy too many apps.

Impulse shop if you're prone to impulse purchases.

 Run a tab.

It's super easy to slide into less-than-ideal spending habits without even noticing. Here are six of the most common budget-busting habits and easy ways to break them.

DOs

 Buy generic. Generics and store brands can cost up to 50% less for virtually the same thing.

 Use "native" ATMs. If your bank doesn't have convenient ATMs, open another account in a bank that does.

Save to buy stock instead—it's still a bit of a gamble, with a better chance of winning.

 Avoid the temptation of low-priced apps and look for free alternatives; also, be mindful of in-app purchases and limit those expenses.

 Start shopping with a reliable accountability buddy or swap shopping with another impulsive buddy and strictly follow each other's lists.

Pay as you go, so you know exactly what you're spending.

When to Pay with...

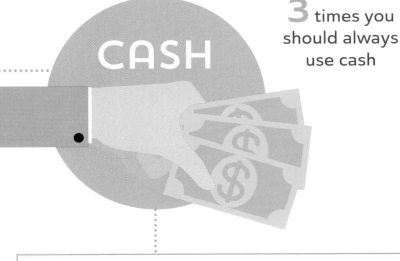

CASH

3 times you should always use cash

1. **BILLS THAT CHARGE FEES** Some recurring bills (like utilities or health insurance premiums) charge a small fee when you pay by credit card, so only use cash for those bills.

2. **PAYING OFF DEBTS** If certain bills (like medical bills) are getting out of hand, negotiate a plan with the creditor, which almost always costs less than paying by credit card and racking up interest.

3. **SMALL, EVERYDAY PURCHASES** Putting daily lattes and lunches on your credit card can land you in debt and stick you with interest payments that end up costing more than the original charges.

Credit card use means you're borrowing money, with a promise to repay the loan, possibly with interest.

Debit card use pulls cash directly and immediately out of your bank account.

Cash use means handing over physical money or paying by check (either paper or through online banking).

When it comes to spending, paying with cash is usually the best bet. But there are times when it makes better financial sense to use a credit card (as long as you handle your credit responsibly and pay off your full balance every month). Make sure you know which features your credit card offers—don't just assume—before making the purchase.

CREDIT

5 times it makes more sense to use a credit card

1. **PRICE PROTECTION** If you buy something and then find the same product for a lower price within ninety days, some credit cards will refund the difference to you, thanks to a card feature called price protection.

2. **EXTENDED WARRANTIES FOR ELECTRONICS** Most credit cards offer automatic extended warranty coverage on electronics and appliances, so you can skip the costly retail version.

3. **HOTEL STAYS AND RENTAL CARS** Paying for these services with cash or a debit card often requires a hefty deposit or a hold on your bank account, making universally accepted credit cards a much easier choice.

4. **INTERNATIONAL TRAVEL** Lost or stolen credit cards are easily replaceable; cash is not.

5. **LARGE PURCHASES** Open a 0% interest store credit card account when you make a large purchase (like a sofa or washer/dryer), as long as you can pay off the purchase during that 0% interest period.

10 EASY WAYS
to Spend Less at Home

If you're having trouble putting together a balanced budget, here are some solid ideas for cutting your expenses at home right now. Each one by itself may not save you tons of money, but if you combine several of them, the savings will add up over time.

1   **TURN THE THERMOSTAT DOWN (OR UP)**

Cut heating and cooling costs by turning your thermostat down one degree in winter and up one degree in summer. One degree—which you probably won't even notice—can save you 3% on your heating and cooling bills, and that could add up to a lot of money in a year.

2   **GET YOUR BOOKS AND MOVIES FROM THE LIBRARY**

From print books and ebooks to audiobooks and movies, your library has a wide range of free entertainment options. And if you're looking for digital media, you can usually do your borrowing from home.

3   **INVEST IN A WATER FILTER**

By switching from bottled water to filtered water using a sink or Brita filter, you can save thousands of dollars every year. Added bonus: drinking filtered water is also better for the environment.

4   **MAKE YOUR OWN CLEANING PRODUCTS**

Mixing up DIY household cleaners is not only easy, it's also a big money saver since you can make them from kitchen staples like vinegar, lemon juice, and baking soda.

5   CUT YOUR CABLE SERVICE

In today's world, you can find news and entertainment right on the Internet. Inexpensive alternatives like Netflix, Hulu, and Amazon Prime give you access to the popular shows and movies that you'd find on cable networks.

6   SWITCH TO LED LIGHT BULBS

It's never been easier to find an affordable LED lighting option. These energy-efficient bulbs last five times longer than incandescent bulbs and can help you save on overall home energy costs.

7   AVOID EXTENDED WARRANTIES

No matter what major purchase you make—car, furnace, computer, or dishwasher—you'll probably be offered an extended warranty by the company selling you the product. Though extended warranties may be a good investment in limited cases, their costs usually outweigh their benefits.

8   SHOP ONLINE AUCTIONS, SALES, AND RESALE SHOPS

Whether you're furnishing a nursery or building a wardrobe, online auctions, tag sales, and resale or consignment shops can save you a bundle while still offering long-lasting, high-quality products.

9   BUY PRODUCE THAT IS FROZEN OR IN SEASON

In-season fruits and vegetables are generally cheaper than out-of-season or exotic produce. You should also consider buying frozen options since they're inexpensive and keep longer than fresh produce.

10   WASH CLOTHES IN COLD WATER

Switch to cold water when doing your laundry to save on energy costs without losing any cleaning power.

WHICH INSURANCE
DO **YOU** NEED?

It's an expense nobody wants until they need it—and then it's too late. Insurance provides a financial safety net for emergencies, covering costs we don't plan on and probably couldn't manage without sinking our savings or going into debt. Which types of policies you need depends on your unique circumstances, but everyone should at least consider these seven policies.

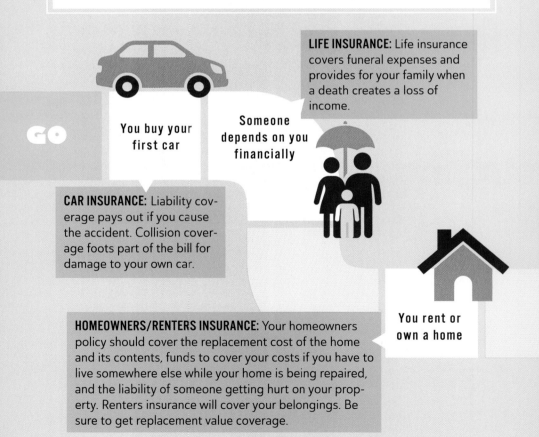

LIFE INSURANCE: Life insurance covers funeral expenses and provides for your family when a death creates a loss of income.

You buy your first car

Someone depends on you financially

GO

CAR INSURANCE: Liability coverage pays out if you cause the accident. Collision coverage foots part of the bill for damage to your own car.

You rent or own a home

HOMEOWNERS/RENTERS INSURANCE: Your homeowners policy should cover the replacement cost of the home and its contents, funds to cover your costs if you have to live somewhere else while your home is being repaired, and the liability of someone getting hurt on your property. Renters insurance will cover your belongings. Be sure to get replacement value coverage.

You're
planning to take
maternity leave
in the next year

You're
worth
enough to
be worth
suing

END

UMBRELLA POLICY: An umbrella policy protects your personal assets from lawsuits and covers your legal fees. So if your dog bites a neighbor or your two-year-old colors on an expensive antique, the umbrella has you covered.

SHORT-TERM DISABILITY: Many workers use short-term disability to cover their maternity leave. This coverage provides a percentage of your salary, and typically is either provided by your employer or purchased as an employee benefit.

You start
earning
income

HEALTH INSURANCE: Medical insurance should cover you for emergencies and routine visits, so accidents and basic care don't dent your budget.

LONG-TERM DISABILITY: LTD replaces a big portion of your income even if you can't work for months or years. Buy coverage that replaces 65% of your current salary.

You're
responsible
for your own
medical bills

COMPLETE CAR

When people buy a car, they focus mainly on the sticker price and the monthly loan payments. But car costs don't stop when you drive off the lot. You'll shell out a lot more money over the life of your car, so remember to take the whole cost into account before you buy.

$1,268
gas

REAL COSTS
for Car Owners

Along with your car payment, be prepared to pay an annual average (according to AAA).

$1,222
insurance

$150
tires

CO$T GUIDE

$792
repairs and
maintenance

$687
registration fees,
licenses, and taxes

NEW VS. USED

New cars lose value the second you buy them. That's why buying a high-quality used car is virtually always a better choice. Also, the type of vehicle plays a big role in ongoing fuel and maintenance costs.

Rule of thumb: the bigger the vehicle, the bigger the price tag for everything.

NEW CAR

AVERAGE LOAN AMOUNT $30,621
AVERAGE MONTHLY PAYMENT $506

USED CAR

AVERAGE LOAN AMOUNT $19,329
AVERAGE MONTHLY PAYMENT $364

HOW MUCH WILL THAT CAR COST YOU?

Before you buy any new or used car, you can estimate the expected total costs for that specific car with Edmunds True Cost to Own (TCO) calculator at www.edmunds.com/tco.html.

Shopping for
CAR INSURANCE:

DOS AND DON'TS

Do get quotes from several insurance companies.

Do ask the insurance company about discounts. Oftentimes they will offer discounts for being a good driver or bundling policies together.

DO

Do ask if you will get a loaner car should you get in an accident.

Do consider paying your policy in full, since it is often less expensive than paying monthly.

Do make sure your current policy reflects your current needs.

Most states require drivers to have auto insurance. But even if it's not required, it's strongly advised to help protect you and your assets. Car insurance is divided into three areas of coverage: collision, comprehensive, and liability. When reviewing policies, be sure they touch on these key areas and that you follow these dos and don'ts.

DON'T

Don't forget to review your driving record before shopping for insurance, since tickets and points can drive up quotes.

Don't forget to ask your employer about discounts. Many companies team up with insurance companies to offer lower rates for employees.

Don't just sign up for the minimum. While minimum coverage will cost you less up front, you will need to pay for damages that go beyond what your policy covers.

Don't be afraid to switch to another company if you find a better deal later on.

Don't buy a lot of unnecessary extras, such as towing insurance.

10 TAX DEDUCTIONS AND CREDITS
YOU'RE PROBABLY FORGETTING

1 STATE AND LOCAL TAXES

You can deduct either the state and local sales taxes or the state and local income taxes you paid. If you live in a state with no (or very low) income tax, it makes sense to go for the sales taxes. Keep records of all the sales tax you've paid to take full advantage of this lucrative deduction.

2 OUT-OF-POCKET CHARITABLE CONTRIBUTIONS

Even if your cash or noncash donation was small, writing it off can really make a difference.

3 TRAVEL VOLUNTEERING

If you volunteer at a qualified charity, you may be able to include your mileage as a tax deduction.

4 JOB-HUNTING COSTS

If you've recently conducted a job search, you may be able to deduct those expenses as long as the search was in the same line of work as your current job.

5 WORK UNIFORMS

You may be able to claim the amount you paid for your uniform and the cost of laundering if your employer doesn't reimburse you.

Filling out your forms properly requires a basic understanding of how taxes work and an awareness of significant tax-reduction opportunities. Here are some tax deductions and credits you may be qualified for but may not have considered.

6 CHILD CARE

If you're a parent of a child under age thirteen or a disabled dependent of any age, you could reduce your tax bill by up to 35% of expenses: up to $3,000 for 1 child (or $6,000 for 2 or more).

7 MORTGAGE INTEREST

If you're a homeowner, you are eligible to fully deduct the interest you paid on your mortgage as long as the loan was $1 million or less ($500,000 or less if you're married and filing separately).

8 COLLEGE CREDIT

You can claim a Lifetime Learning Credit of up to $2,000 for qualified education expenses as long as your modified adjusted gross income is less than $65,000.

9 INVESTMENT FEES AND EXPENSES

If you pay for investment counseling, broker commissions, or custodial fees, all of your investment-related expenses can be deducted as "miscellaneous expenses" on your Schedule A.

10 TAX PREPARATION FEES

You may be able to deduct tax preparation fees whether you did them yourself or paid someone to do them for you. These fees get included in the "miscellaneous deductions" section of Schedule A.

5 STEPS to Effectively Freeze Your Spending

If your spending is getting the best of you, try freezing your spending on wants (as opposed to needs) for the next several months. Freezing your spending isn't easy, but it can stop your accelerating debt dead in its tracks.

4

3

2

1

5

Put Away Your Credit and Debit Cards

Put your credit and debit cards in a safe place that's hard to get to, such as a safe-deposit box at the bank. The farther away your credit and debit cards are from you, the better. You'll also need to delete any saved card information online so you can't buy anything without having the card in front of you. Then, during your freeze period, pay for all of your day-to-day purchases with cash and pay your bills with checks.

Stick to Your Shopping List

Before you leave the house and head out to spend money, write down a shopping list of your needs. Then buy only the items on the list. If you see something you absolutely need that isn't on your list, put it on next week's list when you get home. Be vigilant about this process, and you'll never overspend on groceries and toiletries again.

Resist Temptation

The best way to stay the course during your freeze is to steer clear of opportunities to spend money. This might mean that you block websites of your favorite e-tailers, avoid shopping plazas, make all your meals at home, or invite friends and family over instead of going out.

Establish What's Really a Need

Understanding the difference between a need and a want is really the crux of sorting out your finances. When it comes to needs, there are very few expenses that fall into the category: shelter, clothing, food and water, and transportation. Of course, every situation is different, and you may have other needs (like child care or Internet access for work). However, anything that isn't a necessity should be cut out of your spending during the freeze.

Decide How Long to Freeze Your Spending

In order to make this spending freeze effective, decide how long you want to carry out this plan. Freezing your spending for six to twelve months can really make a difference and help you get back on track.

HIDDEN COSTS
and how to avoid them

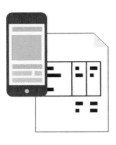

CELL PHONE BILL

Cell phone bills pack in a lot of sneaky charges, many of them for services that you don't really need or want. Save money by scrutinizing your bill for those unwanted charges.

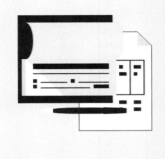

COST	HOW TO AVOID IT	COST
Bloated data plan	Review your data usage. Don't pay for more data than you really need every month. But if you're consistently using too much data, it's cheaper to upgrade your data plan than to keep paying high overage fees.	Monthly maintenance fees
Monthly phone payments	Pay for your phone up front. Phone payment plans often end up costing substantially more than the retail price of the phone. You can get better deals on *Amazon* and *eBay*.	Overdraft fees
Early upgrades	Unless you really need a new smartphone every year, it doesn't pay to upgrade that often; so cut the very costly early upgrade add-on fee.	Foreign transaction fees

Hidden costs can bump up your expenses and drain your budget. Take control by ferreting out these sneaky fees and taking simple steps to avoid them.

CHECKING ACCOUNT

Bank fees add up very quickly, and if you aren't expecting them, they can even lead to overdrafts (and more fees). Here's how you can eliminate common bank fees.

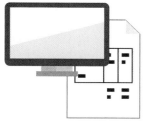

CABLE BILL

Cable companies are notorious for hidden and confusing fees. Here are some tips to help cut that cable bill down to size.

HOW TO AVOID IT	COST	HOW TO AVOID IT
Keep a minimum balance in your account or have your paycheck direct-deposited into the account.	Hidden fees in the introductory deal	Read the fine print on your "great" introductory deal to dig out the extra fees not mentioned in that low bundle price. That deal may not be your best choice after all.
Keep track of your outstanding checks, automatic payments, direct debits (like from PayPal), ATM withdrawals, debit card transactions, and bank fees so you always know your true checking account balance.	Equipment rental	Cable companies typically charge you every month for every remote, cable box, and DVR. Save hundreds of dollars a year by limiting your equipment rental or buying what you need.
These fees crop up when you travel overseas, even if you pay for things in US dollars. Avoid these bank fees by using a credit card that doesn't charge them.	Taxes, fees, and surcharges	Since these fees vary by provider, shop around for the one with the lowest charges.
	Paying more than new customers	Use a different phone than the one attached to your account (so they can't tell what you already have) to call the company and ask for their best deals.

7 TIPS FOR SPENDING LESS ON YOUR GROCERY BILL

Whether or not you shop the sales, you can find additional ways to cut a bit here and a bit there when it comes to your grocery bill. You'd be surprised how much those savings can really add up when you carefully look at what you're purchasing and how you use those items at home. Here are a few tips to help you trim costs when you're planning your meals and considering a trip to the grocery store.

4 Check Apps for Deals

Write out your shopping list. Then look through that week's advertisements, noting on your list which store has the best prices on the items you need.

5 Buy Sale Items in Quantity

If you see a great sale price on a nonperishable item that you use a lot, stock up at the sale price.

1 Cook from Scratch

One way to save hundreds of dollars every month is by making your own food versus buying frozen or prepared foods.

2 Think about Your Food Choices

Cereal is considered a staple of the American diet. But ounce for ounce, it's one of the most expensive foods in your grocery store! Consider what changes you can make to help your wallet without hurting your diet.

3 Use Coupons and Get Discounts

Every year, consumers save $4 billion with coupons! This free money can help you stick to your budget, but only if you use it for products you would have purchased anyway.

6 Join a Wholesale Club

One way to get sale prices every day is to shop at a wholesale club. Make sure you're saving more money than the annual membership fee, and don't overspend in the name of a good deal.

7 Grow a Garden, Even a Small One

If you eat a lot of veggies, you know they can be expensive. Yet for just a few dollars for the seeds, you can grow an entire garden of fresh vegetables every year. You can even freeze or can them for use in the cold months.

CHAPTER 3
DEBT AND CREDIT

3 STEPS TO SHOP FOR THE PERFECT CREDIT CARD FOR YOU

1 IDENTIFY YOUR NEEDS

There are many types of credit cards available, so think about the features that mesh with your financial goals. Some cards aim to help improve damaged credit, others offer low rates that let you save money on interest, and still others offer a variety of rewards. Here are some things to consider:

- **INTEREST RATE:** If you will potentially carry a balance on your card, pick a lower interest rate.

- **CREDIT LIMIT:** Is the card for emergencies, or will you be using it for everyday purchases? Make sure the credit limit reflects how much you'll be spending on the card.

- **PENALTIES:** These are less important if you know you can pay off your card in full each month, but if you might carry a balance it's smart to be aware of what you'll be getting into for late fees and other penalties.

From the usual suspects like Visa and Mastercard to department stores and online retailers like Amazon, it seems like everyone is offering their own credit cards. Although many credit card companies offer special services, it is worth your while to explore your options and seek out credit cards that work best for you and your needs. Follow these steps to narrow your search.

2 HONE IN ON THE BENEFITS

Now you can really dig into how different credit card companies will help you achieve your financial goals. For instance, if you want to minimize interest payments, research the card's balance transfer policy and its ongoing interest APR (annual percentage rate). If you're looking for rewards, pick a card that offers the highest rewards for items that you're already purchasing, and make sure those are the rewards you really want. If you're tracking your credit, consider a card that offers free monthly FICO score reporting.

You can find cards that offer benefits for making specific purchases, like:

- **GROCERIES**
- **GAS**
- **RETAIL ITEMS**
- **HOTELS AND TRAVEL**

Others will offer specific rewards for spending, like:

- **GIFT CARDS**
- **DISCOUNTS**
- **CASH BACK**
- **AIRLINE MILES**

3 APPLY FOR THE CREDIT CARD WITH THE BEST VALUE

Once you've narrowed down your options to just a couple of credit cards, it's time to choose. Look closely at each card and decide which one offers the best overall value for you and your financial goals.

STRATEGIES
FOR DEALING WITH
STUDENT LOAN DEBT

Millions of people struggle every month to make their student loan payments. If your student loans are weighing you down, check out these ways you can lighten the load.

LOWER YOUR INTEREST RATE

Most student loan servicers will automatically lower your rate by 0.25% if you sign up for automatic payments.

ASK ABOUT DEFERMENT AND FORBEARANCE

Put your payments, but not interest, on pause. If your lender allows it, you can choose between making monthly interest payments and stopping all payments and having the interest that builds during that period added to your total loan balance.

CHANGE YOUR REPAYMENT PLAN

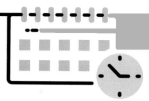

These six repayment plans are available in addition to the standard plan. Visit www.studentaid.gov for information about eligibility and more details.

▷▷ Graduated: Payments are lower in the beginning, and then increase every two years for up to ten years.

▷▷ Extended: Offers a longer loan term—up to twenty-five years—and lower monthly payments, which can be fixed or graduated.

▷▷ Pay As You Earn (PAYE)*: Maximum monthly payment is 10% of discretionary income, and loan term is extended to twenty years.

▷▷ Revised Pay As You Earn (REPAYE)*: Monthly payment equals 10% of discretionary income, and loan term is extended to twenty years.

▷▷ Income-Based Repayment (IBR)*: Monthly payment equals 10% or 15% of discretionary income, depending on when your loan originated. Loan term is extended for up to twenty-five years.

▷▷ Income-Contingent Repayment (ICR)*: Monthly payment equals the lesser of 20% of discretionary income or what a fixed payment would be on a twelve-year loan. Loan term is extended for up to twenty-five years.

> *Payments for income-driven repayment plans are recalculated every year based on updated income and current family size, along with other factors.

CONSOLIDATE AND REFINANCE

Roll all of your loans into one with a lower interest rate; this means more of your payment goes toward principal every month. However, you lose some of the protections built in to your federal student loans, including access to repayment plans.

THE DOs & DON'Ts
of Using Credit Cards

DOs

✓ Review your credit card statements regularly to keep your purchases in check.

✓ Pay your bill on time to avoid late fee charges.

✓ Pay off your full balance every month to avoid paying interest.

✓ Reduce your credit card limit if you're tempted to overspend.

✓ Take advantage of rewards programs.

✓ Protect yourself against credit card fraud.

There's no question about it: credit cards make life more convenient, but not necessarily easier. If you overuse them, they can become the biggest obstacle to reaching your financial goals. To get the most out of your cards, and avoid being trapped by credit card debt, consider these valuable tips.

DON'TS

 Use a credit card to make ends meet.

 Own more than five credit cards at one time.

 Pick the first credit card you see. Thoroughly research different options before making a decision.

 Exceed 25% of your credit line, since your debt may start to affect your credit score.

 Use rewards programs as an excuse to buy more.

Make large purchases with your credit card unless you can pay the full balance immediately.

When to Transfer Credit Card Balances

If you have a lot of high interest rate–credit card debt, a balance transfer could help you pay it off faster and save a lot of money, as long as you do it the right way.

How It Works

You get a new credit card with a 0% introductory interest rate, and transfer your old, high-rate balance onto the new card.

Dos and Don'ts

DO	DON'T
Look for a card with no fee for balance transfers	Cancel your old card (that could hurt your credit score)
Find a card with an introductory rate period of at least twelve months	Run up new debt on your old credit card
Pay off your transferred debt before the introductory period expires	Miss or be late with a single payment or you'll lose the 0% rate
Strictly limit new purchases on your old card to what you can pay off immediately	Use your new credit card for new purchases (payments will go toward them first, and not toward your transfer)

A LOOK AT SOME NUMBERS

A $5,000 credit card balance on a card with a 13.99% interest rate, while paying just the *minimum* monthly payment of $150, would take:

43 MONTHS
(3.6 YEARS)
to pay off

and cost $1,368 in interest

Transfer that $5,000 to a card with a 0% interest rate for twenty-four months, paying $208 per month, and it would take:

24 MONTHS
to pay off

and cost $0 in interest

WHAT'S IN A CREDIT SCORE?

Your credit score affects your life in more ways than you may realize, so it's crucial to know your number. A less-than-desirable score can keep you out of your dream house, spike the interest rate on new credit cards, and get you passed over for your perfect job. Knowing your score—and what goes into calculating it—can help you build better credit.

Poor   Excellent

✓ Credit Check

Credit scores are not the same as credit reports. Your credit score is a number that lets creditors know—at a glance—how likely you are to pay your debts. Your credit report holds the detailed story of your entire credit history and your current credit situation.

Contrary to popular belief, checking your credit has no impact on your credit score. Your score can be affected when other people (like potential lenders or landlords) look at your credit.

OLDER AND CREDIT-WISER

It probably won't come as a surprise that credit scores tend to grow as we get older. Here's how average credit scores vary by age in the US.

21–34	634
35–49	655
50–69	700
70 and older	730

5 Factors Set the Score

There are many different credit-scoring systems around the world—even inside the US. And while the numbers can look really different, they're mainly calculated based on these five factors.

1 ### Payment history

Whether or not you pay your bills on time or at all

2 ### Total outstanding debt

How much you owe right now

3 ### Credit types

Your credit mix (for example, a mortgage and a car loan and credit card debt)

4 ### Length of credit history

How long you've had credit

5 ### Credit applications history

The number of times you've tried to get credit (whether or not you were successful)

HOW TO ESTABLISH
CREDIT

You need a credit history to get credit, and you can't get credit without a credit history. If no one will give you credit, how should you develop a history of responsibly paying your debts?

THE TRICK TO ESTABLISHING GOOD CREDIT IS TO MAKE SURE YOU PAY EVERY BILL AND MAKE EVERY PAYMENT ON TIME.

TIPS

Don't go into debt to build your credit.

An "excellent" credit rating takes up to seven years to build. An "average" or "good" rating can be built in one or two years.

A credit report details the past. A credit score predicts your future credit behavior.

Here are some solutions to this predicament—specific tools you can use to help you build a credit history from scratch:

Secured credit cards

Backed by cash deposits, secured credit cards give you a chance to borrow and pay back money with a safety net. They work exactly like regular credit cards and come with the same payment responsibilities. Once you've established credit, cancel the secured card and get your deposit back.

Authorized user status

Someone who trusts you may be willing to add you on to his or her credit card as an "authorized user." You'll be able to use the card and establish credit history without the full legal obligation to pay the bills (make sure you and the cardholder have a clear understanding to avoid future problems). Before you go this route, make sure the credit card company reports authorized user activity to the credit reporting agencies (most do).

Credit-builder loans

These small loans—usually offered by community banks and credit unions—exist to help people establish credit, and they work sort of like secured credit cards. You have to "repay" the loan—by depositing money into a savings account—before you're allowed to borrow any money. Once you do borrow the money and pay it all back, the lender reports your good (or bad, if you miss payments) credit behavior to the credit bureaus.

HOW TO REPAIR
Bad Credit

Bad credit can affect your life in a lot of ways, often limiting your options to a frustrating degree: you can get turned down for credit cards and loans (or have higher interest rates on those you do get), and get turned away from job opportunities, apartments, and even things like life insurance. Increasing your credit score, and moving it into the "good" category, unlocks financial (and personal) opportunities. There's no instant fix; repairing bad credit takes time. By taking four simple steps, you can raise your credit score out of the undesirable zone in about three to six months.

A 4-Step Plan to Repair Your Credit

No matter how bad your credit is, you can repair it. By taking these four steps, you can improve your credit score in just a few months.

1 **Get a free copy of your credit report.**

Everyone is entitled to one free credit report every year from each of the Big Three credit-reporting agencies. The most reputable source for obtaining your free credit reports is www.annualcreditreport.com. Once you read your credit report, you'll have a firm starting point.

Credit Check

Soft inquiries—like when you check your own credit or get a "preapproved" credit application in the mail—don't affect your credit score. Hard inquiries, such as credit checks by lenders or employers, do affect your score.

2 Fix mistakes.

An estimated 25–30% of credit reports contain mistakes, so look yours over carefully. If you find any errors, dispute them immediately, either through the reporting agency's online dispute process, or by sending a letter to both the credit reporting agency and the creditor involved.

3 Pay down big credit card balances.

Credit utilization (your current credit card balance in relation to your credit limit) plays a huge role in your credit score. Maxed-out cards will keep your credit score in the basement. Paying down balances as quickly as possible will lift it up fast.

CREDIT CARD STATEMENT

4 Pay every bill on time, every time.

Missed payments haunt your credit report for seven years—and the reporting agencies can't tell (and don't care) whether you missed a payment because you forgot to pay or because you couldn't pay. And even one skipped payment can take a one hundred point toll on your score.

THE BIG THREE: EQUIFAX, EXPERIAN, AND TRANSUNION

These are the three major credit reporting companies in the US. Each one reports your credit history in a slightly different format. Different potential creditors can look at information from all three, or just one.

EVERYTHING YOU NEED
TO KNOW ABOUT YOUR
DEBT-TO-INCOME RATIO

When you're looking to borrow money, you'll need to know your debt-to-income ratio, or DTI. Your debt-to-income ratio is a percentage calculated by dividing your total recurring monthly debt by your monthly gross income. Your DTI reveals how well you can manage your debt. Lenders—especially mortgage lenders—look at this number when they're deciding whether you can borrow money and how much.

**When it comes to DTI,
the lower the better.**

Below 20% . . . . EXCELLENT

20% to 40% . . . . . . AVERAGE

40% to 50% . . . . . . STRESSED

Over 50% . . . . DANGER

Figure out your DTI with this formula:

[Monthly Debt] / [Monthly Gross Income] = DTI%

For example:

Monthly gross income	$4,500
Mortgage or rent payment	$1,000
Student loan payment	$240
Car loan or lease payment	$400
Credit card payment	$100
Total monthly debt payments	$1,740
DTI ($1,740 / $4,500)	38.7%

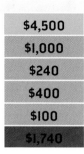

Gross or Net?

A lot of people ask why DTI uses gross income instead of net income (the amount you actually take home). Lenders use the gross because it's both comparable and stable: people may have different payroll deductions, and those are more likely to change during the year than salary. For a truer picture of your DTI, use your net income in the calculation.

HOW TO DIG

When your finances are crushed under a mountain of debt, it can be hard to imagine a way out. This is one of those times when a big-picture view won't help you. To dig your way out of this financial mess, you need to go smaller and focus on one debt at a time.

SNOWBALL

The snowball method starts small and grows bigger—the payoffs "snowball" over time. That's because when you pay off a debt, all the money you were using to pay it goes toward the next debt, so those monthly payments get bigger. To use this method, list all of your debts in order of size, from the smallest balance to the largest. The smallest debt on the list is your focus debt; when it's paid off, the new smallest debt becomes the focus, until there is no more.

GRAB YOUR SHOVEL

Whichever method you choose, a few basic features are the same:

- Make minimum payments every month on every debt.
- Choose one debt to focus on for early payoff.
  - Use any extra cash you have to make dents in the focus debt.
    - As soon as that debt is paid off, shift the focus to the next one.
    - Repeat the process until every debt is paid off entirely.

BOTTOM LINE:
It doesn't matter which method you use. By focusing on

OUT OF DEBT

You have two main choices here—**SNOWBALL** and **AVALANCHE**—to help you chip away at that solid block of debt just a little bit faster.

AVALANCHE

Under the avalanche method, you tackle the most expensive debt first by focusing on whichever debt comes with the highest interest rate, no matter what the balance due is. The idea here is that chipping away at high-interest debt lets you pay out less interest overall. To use this method, list all of your debts in order of interest rate, from highest to lowest; the top-rate debt is your focus debt until they're all paid down.

SNOWBALL VS. AVALANCHE: WHICH WORKS BEST FOR YOU?

If math were the only factor, the avalanche method would win every time. By focusing on high interest-rate debts first, you end up paying less interest over time and pay down your debts a little faster. For many people, though, the satisfaction of seeing the first debts paid off quickly under the snowball method gives them the motivation to keep going. The obvious progress keeps them on track and helps create the pay-down habit, making it easier to stick to the plan when larger debts become the focus.

one debt at a time, you'll be able to pay off all of them.

WHAT TO DO IF YOU'RE A VICTIM OF
IDENTITY THEFT OR CREDIT CARD FRAUD

If someone's been using your identity to trash your finances and your credit, there's a lot you can do to set the record straight. Take immediate action so you won't be on the hook for the fraudulent charges and your credit can be repaired quickly.

It can be tricky to know when someone's stolen your identity or committed financial fraud against you. Here are some clues to look for:

HOW WILL YOU KNOW?

Some of your bills or other pieces of mail go missing

There are unfamiliar charges on your credit card statement

Money is missing from your bank account

You get calls from debt collectors about debts that aren't yours

You go to e-file your tax return and it gets rejected

You get medical bills that aren't yours

STEPS TO TAKE IF THIS HAPPENS TO YOU

Contact your credit card companies and bank, let them know you're a fraud victim, and tell them which charges are fraudulent.

Get free copies of all of your credit reports.

Go to each credit reporting company's website to view your credit reports online and dispute every account and charge that does not belong to you.

Place a free ninety-day fraud alert on one of your credit reports (Experian, TransUnion, or Equifax), and that company is required to notify the other two for you.

File a police report.

Visit IdentityTheft.gov to file an Identity Theft Affidavit (a sworn statement) and create an Identity Theft Report (you'll need the police report number to complete this).

Verify that the fraud alert was placed (this can take up to a week to appear).

CHAPTER 4
INVESTING

The Path to **INVESTING**

Investing may seem like a daunting process, but the sooner you start, the easier it will be to build a big enough nest egg to make life easier in the future. Since investing always includes some risk, it's important to have a solid financial foundation before you begin. Go through this list to make sure you're ready to invest.

1
You have a steady income.

2
You have money left over after meeting your financial obligations.

6
You know your risk tolerance.

7
You've set realistic expectations for investment returns.

3

You've considered the effect of upcoming personal changes, such as marriage, children, or divorce, before investing.

4

You've built up your savings, including a three- to six-month emergency fund, before establishing an investment capital fund.

5

You did your homework before investing in anything.

8

You've developed a diversified investment plan.

You're Ready to Invest!

HOW TO **Research** STOCKS

STEP 1

Look to the Past

Numbers don't lie: you can see how the company did last year by looking at its financial statements, which you can find online. These statements include:

- A balance sheet (a listing of what the company owns and owes)
- A statement of profit and loss (a summary of the company's sales and expenses)
- A statement of cashflows (a look at how money flowed in and out of the company)

What indicates that a stock might be a good bet? A company that owns more than it owes, has strong sales and solid profits, and has more cash coming in from operations than from loans.

STEP 2

Look to the Future

Every year, public corporations publish annual reports to look back at the past year's performance and talk about the company's future prospects.

A company with strong future growth potential might include:

- Plans to expand into new markets
- Robust research and development
- New products on the horizon
- Sensible acquisitions

Buying a stock means buying a piece of a company, and that calls for some research. When you're investing, you're looking for future growth and income, so you want to make sure the companies you buy into have that potential. To do that you should look at the company's past successes (or failures), projections for the future, and the overall trend of the stock's performance.

STEP 3

Look at Trends

In addition to recent successes and solid outlooks, you want to make sure that stocks you purchase have consistently performed well and improved year over year. For this, you need to look at the stock's performance trends.

Online stock trackers like *Yahoo! Finance* and *The Wall Street Journal* offer extensive information on every stock out there. All you need is the company's ticker symbol (its abbreviated name, like MSFT for Microsoft) and you can find a wealth of data, including the historical stock price. Other key numbers to check out include the P/E ratio (price-to-earnings ratio) and EPS (earnings per share). Look for growing stock prices and EPS, and a falling or steady P/E ratio.

Other Information Sources:

EDGAR (Electronic Data Gathering, Analysis, and Retrieval) is a comprehensive database created by the US Securities and Exchange Commission (SEC) that holds all corporate reports filed by public companies and complaints filed against the companies—all the way back through 1994.

Value Line provides data, rankings, and insights into thousands of stocks. The website also offers decision-making tools to help investors choose among the stocks they're interested in.

Nasdaq offers up-to-the-minute and historical stock quotes, plus overall market performance statistics. The website also provides a stock screening tool, so you can narrow down stocks that might fit into your portfolio.

Different Ways

You've decided to invest in the stock market. Now you have two main actions to take: choosing a broker and placing your first order to buy stock (once you own stock, you'll be able to place orders to sell stock as well).

CHOOSE A BROKER TYPE

There are three basic types of brokers you can use when you want to buy stocks.

1 ▶ Full-service brokers

- Charge the most and highest fees.
- Offer a wide range of financial planning services and advice (including which stocks to buy and sell).
- Often receive commissions on your trades (so make sure their recommendations fit your financial plan).

2 ▶ Discount brokers

- Charge reduced trading fees (flat fees that are charged per trade, regardless of the number of shares traded or their price).
- Don't offer financial advice.
- Let you place your orders online or with a person who will walk you through the order if you need support.

3 ▶ Online-only brokers

- Typically charge the lowest fees.
- Don't offer live financial advice; may offer robo-advisers.
- Let you place orders directly whenever you want to buy or sell stock.

to Buy Stock

You have a few different options when it comes to the type of broker you want to work with, and also some flexibility in how you place your stock orders.

CHOOSE AN ORDER TYPE

There are two main ways to place orders to buy or sell stock.

1 ▶ Market order

You buy or sell stock at whatever the current market price is when your order hits the trading floor (not necessarily the moment you place the order).

EXAMPLE: You place a market order to buy 100 shares of ABC Corp. Your order goes through immediately, and you pay the current price for your shares, whatever that may be.

2 ▶ Limit order

You set a maximum buying price or minimum selling price for your order. Limit orders cost more to place than market orders.

EXAMPLE: You place a limit order to buy 100 shares of ABC Corp. for no more than $9 per share. Your order won't be placed until the stock price drops to $9 or below.

The Path to Choosing a
FINANCIAL ADVISER

You may want to see a financial adviser to help you chart a course for the future, or you may want to consult with one at a big turning point in your life. Whatever your reason, choosing the right financial adviser is a decision that shouldn't be taken lightly. Here are some steps to finding one who works for you and your specific needs.

Ask for Recommendations

See if family, friends, or coworkers have any recommendations for great financial advisers.

Research Your Candidates

Industry organizations like NAPFA.org, FINRA.org, and SEC.gov can also tell you more about your candidates and their experience.

Set Up an Initial Appointment

Select your favorite candidate and make an appointment to see them. Learn about their background, how they have helped other clients, what those clients are like, and how this relationship can benefit you.

Review Your Relationship

Take some time to evaluate your relationship with your financial adviser and their firm. How are you working together? Is there anything you wish was different?

Stay in Touch

While you may decide to hire your financial adviser for a specific task or event, it's important to stay in contact throughout the year in order to get the most out of your relationship.

5 Key Benefits of Index Funds

An index fund holds all of the securities (such as stocks or bonds) that are included in a particular market index. Index investing grows more popular every year, as more people take advantage of the many benefits this relaxed style offers. In fact, this strategy has proven profitable for millions of investors just like you.

▼ GOOD STARTER INDEX FUNDS

SPY: SPDR S&P 500 ETF TRUST; TRACKS THE S&P 500 INDEX • **VTSMX:** VANGUARD TOTAL STOCK MARKET INDEX FUND INVESTOR SHARES; MUTUAL FUND TRACKING THE TOTAL US STOCK MARKET • **IEMG:** ISHARES CORE

1 **Passive management:** Index funds—whether they're mutual funds or ETFs (exchange-traded funds)—are set up to follow specific market indexes, in contrast to actively managed funds, where financial professionals choose the fund's holdings.

2 **Unbeatable returns:** Actively managed funds try to beat the market—but they usually don't. To measure their performance, those active funds compare themselves to a comparable index, and more than 80% of the time the index wins. That's also a win for index investors, because index fund returns almost always beat active fund returns.

3 **Low cost:** Index funds have lower expense ratios than managed funds, and that translates into bigger returns for investors. That's because even though the expense percentages seem very small, their negative impact on your returns can be huge. For example, if your fund had 7% returns, a 0.70% expense ratio would eat up 10% of your profits!

4 **Broad holdings:** Typical index funds invest in hundreds, sometimes thousands, of securities—many more than most actively managed funds. That broad exposure helps balance risk for a smoother ride on the market rollercoaster than more targeted funds could achieve.

5 **Tax simplicity:** Index funds buy and sell holdings much less often than actively managed funds. Fewer trades mean fewer taxable transactions—and a lower tax bill for you.

MSCI EMERGING MARKETS ETF; TRACKS THE MSCI (MORGAN STANLEY CAPITAL INTERNATIONAL) EMERGING MARKETS INDEX • **VTWO:** VANGUARD RUSSELL 2000 ETF; TRACKS THE RUSSELL 2000 INDEX

DIFFERENT KINDS OF BONDS
& HOW TO BUY THEM

US GOVERNMENT BONDS
There are two main types of US government bonds.

Treasuries

US savings bonds

Treasuries and US savings bonds are sold to help pay down the national debt and other federal government projects (like infrastructure repairs).

Advantage: interest earned on US government bonds is exempt from state and local income taxes, making them good choices for both retirement and non-retirement investment accounts.

Treasuries pay interest every six months, and include:

- Treasury notes, which have maturity dates ranging from two to ten years
- Treasury bonds, which have thirty-year maturities
- TIPS (Treasury Inflation-Protected Securities), which come with five-year, ten-year, or thirty-year maturities

US savings bonds don't make regular interest payments. Instead, these bonds are sold for less than their face value (for example, you pay $25 for a $50 bond), and you get the full face value back when cashing them in.

They include:

- Series EE bonds, which offer tax breaks when used to pay for higher education expenses
- Series I bonds, which offer inflation protection for interest rates (if inflation increases, so does the interest rate)

You can buy any kind of US bond by visiting www.treasurydirect.gov.

When you buy a bond, you're actually lending money to the bond issuer (the borrower). The issuer pays you a fee—called interest—for the loan, and promises to pay back the full amount (called the face value) on a specific date (called the maturity date). Most bonds have a face value of $1,000. There are several different kinds of bonds available to invest in, and a few different ways to buy them.

MUNICIPAL BONDS

Municipal bonds provide funding for state and local government projects, like building schools and hospitals and repairing roadways.

Advantage: these bonds are exempt from federal income tax, and usually exempt from state income taxes as well, making them a good choice for non-retirement investment accounts.

You can buy municipal bonds:

- Directly from state and local governments
- Through a full-service or online broker
- Through a municipal bond mutual fund or exchange-traded fund

CORPORATE BONDS

Corporate bonds are issued by companies, and generally pay higher interest than government bonds. That higher interest is because there's a higher risk that the company won't be able to pay the principal and interest as stated. Interest is usually paid out semiannually.

Advantage: corporate bonds usually pay higher interest; however, all of the interest earned on corporate bonds is subject to state and federal income taxes, making these a good choice for retirement account investments.

You can buy corporate bonds:

- Through a full-service or online broker
- Through a corporate bond mutual fund or exchange-traded fund

RATING THE RISK

Bonds, whether they're issued by governments or corporations, come with ratings (sort of like your credit rating). Bonds with an AAA rating are the safest, meaning they are the most likely to pay principal and interest in full and on time. Bonds with a C rating (the lowest) are considered high risk, and may be likely to default.

4 WAYS

TO SUPERSIZE YOUR
401(k) NEST EGG

Save for tomorrow and get a big tax break today by contributing as much as possible to your 401(k). To get the biggest benefits out of your employer-sponsored retirement plan, take these four steps...and watch your nest egg supersize before your eyes.

1 Take full advantage of employer matching

If your employer matches 401(k) contributions, cash in. The trick: you have to contribute to get the match. If you don't, you'll be leaving free money on the table.

2 Contribute the max

Right now, you can put $18,000 in your 401(k) every year. And if you're 50 or older, you can sock away an extra $6,000 catch-up contribution, for a total of $24,000 annually. Contribution limits can change from year to year, so make sure to keep track.

3 Start sooner to supercharge growth

Thanks to the power of compounding, the sooner you start stashing a portion of your paycheck in a 401(k), the more money you'll end up with—even if you contribute the same as or less than someone starting later. Here, the early bird gets the biggest nest egg.

SAVE UNTIL/RETIRE AT AGE 67

Starting age	Monthly contributions	Annual contributions	Total contributions	Savings at age 67 (retirement age)
20	$1,000	$12,000	$564,000	$3,663,241
30	$1,500	$18,000	$666,000	$2,422,098
40	$1,500	$18,000	$486,000	$1,434,558
50	$2,000	$24,000	$408,000	$791,976

4 Diversify your investments

Don't put all of your eggs in one basket. Choose a mix of investments to boost returns and minimize risk.

HOW TO CALCULATE YOUR
INVESTMENT RETURNS

Want to know how your investments are performing? All it takes is a little math to find out your ROI (return on investment).

STOCKS

Stocks are equity securities, meaning that each share of stock represents partial ownership of a corporation.

You need **3** numbers to calculate your return on a stock:

1 The total purchase price (price you paid, including any commissions)

2 The total amount of dividends you earned (if any)

3 The current stock price (or the price you sold for) times the number of shares you have

THE FORMULA: [(current stock price − purchase price) + dividends earned] / [purchase price]

EXAMPLE:
Purchase price including commission: $20 per share x 100 shares = $2,000
Dividends earned: $100
Current price: $24 per share x 100 shares = $2,400
ROI: [($2,400 - $2,000) + $100] / $2,000 = 25% return

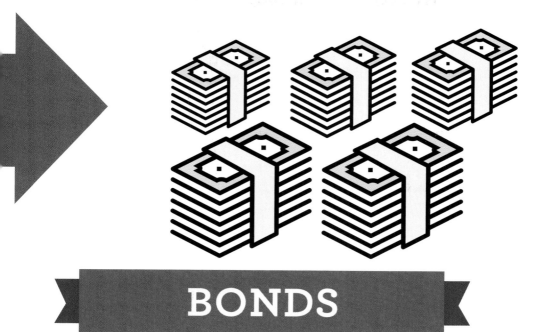

BONDS

Bonds are debt securities, meaning that each bond represents a loan to a government or a corporation.

You need 2 **numbers to calculate your return on a bond:**

1 The total purchase price (price you paid, including any transaction fees)

2 The total amount of interest you earned

THE FORMULA: [interest earned] / [total purchase price]

EXAMPLE:
Price paid for bond: $1,000
Interest received: $30
ROI: $30 / $1,000 = 3% return

6 WAYS THE ECONOMY AFFECTS YOUR PORTFOLIO

The state of the economy (how a country uses money and resources to produce goods and services) greatly affects stock market activity. Whether the economy is growing, shrinking, or standing still, it influences stock performance. To understand the impact of the economy on your portfolio, it helps to see how different economic factors affect stock prices.

With a BULL MARKET, investor confidence is high and stock prices rise, as most stock holdings will increase in value.

With a BEAR MARKET, investors are nervous, stock prices decrease, and many stocks are undervalued. This can also be an opportunity to scoop up good companies for bargain-basement stock prices.

When there is a MARKET BUBBLE, investments are overvalued and their prices are much higher than they're actually worth. Once people realize that stocks (or other investments) cost too much, the bubble "bursts," and prices plummet dramatically. This can be disastrous for portfolios where the investor bought in at the highest price and was still holding those investments when prices hit rock bottom.

 When there is INFLATION, prices are rising and purchasing power is falling ($1 buys less than it used to). But when inflation spikes too high, people can't afford to buy as much as they could before, and corporations may start to lose sales, causing stock prices to drop. This can create a drop in investment values.

 When there is LOW INFLATION, this can indicate a healthy economy, which can be good for the stock market and stock prices.

 **GDP** or gross domestic product, measures the economy as a whole, and lets us know if it's growing or shrinking.

 When INTEREST RATES increase, stock prices tend to decrease; however, some types of corporations (such as banks and mortgage companies) fare better when rates increase, and so do their stock prices. When interest rates drop, stock prices usually rise.

INTEREST RATES ARE SET BY THE FEDERAL RESERVE (A GOVERNMENT AGENCY).

HOW TO MANAGE
Your 401(k)

Many employers offer 401(k) retirement savings plans to their employees. If you're taking advantage of your employer's plan, you've made a great investment in your future. But if you're like most people, you signed up, set it up, and then just forgot about it. Here are some tips on the best ways to manage your 401(k) to get the absolute most from it.

Reevaluate and Rebalance

Once a year, take a look at your asset allocations (the percent of your holdings in stocks and bonds, for example) and make sure that they still fit your overall financial plan:

- If your tolerance for risk has decreased—as it does for most people as they get older—allocate more of your funds toward bonds and safe assets, and fewer to the stock market.

- If investment performance has thrown your allocation balance off (if, for example, a great year in the stock market has caused your stock holdings to grow in value while your bond holdings stayed still), rebalance your holdings (sell off stock or purchase additional bonds) to get back to the allocation you planned.

Roll Over the Right Way

When you change jobs (for whatever reason), you can take your 401(k) with you through a rollover, which really just moves your account from one retirement plan to another. To make sure you don't accidentally trigger a huge tax bill, request a direct rollover when you're ready to make the switch:

- If your new employer offers a 401(k) plan, you can move your account from your former employer directly into it.

- When that's not an option, you can open an IRA and ask your former employer to roll over your 401(k) funds into that.

- The most important thing to remember: don't get the rollover check in your name, or the IRS takes a mandatory 20% withholding tax. Plus, if you don't get that money into another retirement account within sixty days, you'll be subject to another 10% tax penalty.

Resist the Temptation to Borrow

Many employers let employees take loans from their 401(k) accounts—avoid doing that, especially if you plan to use the money to pay off debts (like credit card bills). Even if you pay yourself back, you'll lose out on all of the income your 401(k) could have earned, and that's time and money you'll never get back.

Plus, if you leave your job for any reason (even if you get fired), that loan would have to be paid back in full immediately, or you would get hit with a 10% tax penalty plus regular income taxes on the entire amount.

CHAPTER 5
HOUSING

RENTING vs. BUYING:
WHAT TO CONSIDER

FOR RENT

- 👍 Initial cost (security deposit plus first month's rent) is lower than buying a home
- 👍 Little or no responsibility for maintenance
- 👍 Easier to move since leases are yearly or month-to-month
- 👎 No tax benefits
- 👎 No control over rent increases
- 👎 Limited by landlord's rules on decor

The much-debated question: is it better to rent or buy a home? While there are some major differences between renting and owning a property, deciding what is right for you really depends on your current lifestyle and what you're looking to get out of your home in the next few years. With this in mind, take a look at the following considerations to figure out which option is best for you.

FOR SALE

Tax deductions for mortgage interest and property taxes 👍

Typically stay in a home for five to ten years 👍

Property builds equity 👍

Free to change decor and landscaping however you please (unless you buy a condo or historic home) 👍

Sense of community, stability, security 👍

Initial cost includes down payment and other fees at the time of closing 👎

Responsible for maintenance 👎

Responsible for property taxes 👎

QUESTIONS TO ASK BEFORE YOU SIGN A LEASE

Once you sign a lease on your new apartment, you're stuck with everything it says, including the fine print. Before you sign, make sure to carefully read over everything in the lease, and make sure you understand the whole document. If there are sections you object to, talk to your landlord about making written changes that you'll both initial.

ASK THE FOLLOWING QUESTIONS BEFORE YOU SIGN:

1. When is the rent due?

2. Is there a grace period for rent payments? (Rent may be due on the 1st with a grace period until the 5th, for example.)

3. How do you pay the rent (online, automatic debits, by check)?

4. What is the fee for late rent payments?

5. How long is the lease? (Most people assume it will be twelve months, but that's not always the case.)

6 What utilities and other services (like pest control or parking spaces) are included in the rent?

7 How often can the rent be raised?

8 Will you be responsible for any routine maintenance (like lawn care)?

9 Who should you call for maintenance issues (like a leaky faucet)?

10 How much notice will you get before the landlord enters your apartment?

11 Is renters insurance required?

12 How much notice will you need to provide before moving out?

13 Are you allowed to sublet the apartment (rent to someone else, such as a roommate or a tenant, while you're away)?

14 Where will the landlord hold your security deposit? (Many states require that deposits be held in separate interest-bearing accounts, and that the tenant receives the interest when the deposit is returned.)

15 Are pet deposits refundable? (Note: some states forbid landlords from charging pet deposits, but that doesn't mean landlords won't still try to collect them.)

KNOW YOUR RIGHTS

To find out more about the state laws governing your lease and your tenant rights, visit RentLaw.com.

THE PATH TO BUYING
YOUR FIRST HOME

Finding the right home and financing it is a major task that takes some time and effort. You must be comfortable both financially and emotionally with the home you choose and the method with which you will pay for it.

GET A PREAPPROVAL

The preapproval process is becoming increasingly important because real-estate agents often do not want to start showing you houses until they know how much house you can afford. Your bank will look over all of your financial records to determine your mortgage preapproval.

WORK WITH A REAL-ESTATE AGENT

A real-estate professional will search for homes that meet your needs, notify you as soon as for-sale homes hit the market, negotiate the deal, pen the contract, and guide you to closing. Make sure to find out the realtor's fees up front.

SEARCH FOR HOMES

Work with your agent to narrow down your choices and decide which homes you'd like to see in person.

CHOOSE A HOME

Once you've looked at potential homes, it's time to choose the one that meets your needs, priorities, and budget.

OBTAIN FUNDING

Since the cost of buying a home includes more than just the home's price tag, find out what exactly you're paying for, as well as what your mortgage options look like.

MAKE AN OFFER

Take a look at everything about the property, from the neighborhood to how long it's been on the market. These details will help you figure out what your offer should be. Once you have an offer, compare it to the asking price to make sure it's reasonable.

CLOSE ON YOUR NEW HOME

After your mortgage has been approved, your signed contract accepted, and its contingencies met, you will be notified of the closing (or settlement) date—that is, when the transfer of title to your new home will take place.

EVALUATING HOME INSPECTION PROBLEMS:
What to Consider

Should you buy a home with problems? That depends on the types of problems you find—and all homes have them. With some faults, you may choose to walk away from the best bargain you have ever seen because of the risks involved (or higher costs down the road); with others, you may have the time, money, and motivation to handle the repairs needed. These lists will help inform your decision to buy or not, now that you know a home's faults.

❌ RED LIGHTS

Any item on this list should be enough to turn you away from your prospective purchase:

- ❌ Unsafe or inadequate drinking water
- ❌ A nonfunctioning or malfunctioning private sewer system (septic tank or cesspool)
- ❌ Location in a floodplain
- ❌ Uneven settling or a buckling foundation
- ❌ Uncontrollable basement water problems

YELLOW LIGHTS

These items indicate a need for caution and potential trouble or costly repairs ahead:

- Peeling, cracking, or bubbling exterior paint
- A roof almost in need of repairs
- Deteriorating gutters and downspouts
- Leaks in the roof at the flashings
- Excessive moisture in the attic due to poor ventilation or inadequate insulation
- Pests (termites, bats, mice, squirrels, or roaches)
- Inadequate electrical service
- Inadequate insulation
- Plumbing pipes or fixtures in need of repair or replacement
- Leaks around the bathtub or under a shower stall
- Windows in need of repair or replacement

GREEN LIGHTS

The following findings on a home inspection report should do nothing to disrupt your confidence in the soundness of your potential purchase:

- An aged or inadequate water heater
- Nonworking appliances
- Hairline settling cracks in the foundation
- Leaky faucets
- Dirt, grime, and eyesore decorations

Understanding
Your
Mortgage Options

Getting a mortgage is one of the biggest financial responsibilities you'll ever take on, so it's critical to understand exactly what you're getting into, and how much it will cost you. Many first-time mortgage holders focus on the monthly payment and miss out on big pieces of the mortgage picture, including the lifetime cost of the loan and its future affordability. Make sure you know the exact path your loan will take, so you can always take care of your mortgage payments without breaking a sweat.

Key Factors

Loan Amount

This is the total amount you'll be borrowing; it is usually the price of the house minus your down payment.

15- or 30-Year Terms

Typical mortgage loans come with either fifteen or thirty-year terms. With a thirty-year loan, you'll have lower monthly payments but pay a higher interest rate and a lot more interest over the life of the loan. Fifteen-year loans have lower interest rates and cost less money over time but come with much bigger monthly payments.

Fixed or Adjustable Interest Rate

There are two main choices when it comes to your mortgage interest rate: fixed or adjustable. With a fixed-rate loan, the interest percentage will be set on day one and never change. The interest percentage for an ARM (adjustable-rate mortgage) loan usually starts out very low—much lower than a comparable fixed-rate loan—but changes periodically, along with your monthly payment.

WHAT IS MORTGAGE INTEREST?

Mortgage interest is the money paid as a fee to the lender that loaned you the money to buy your house. The interest rate is the percentage charged on the total outstanding loan balance. The interest payment is included in your monthly mortgage payment, and the dollar amount of the interest payment changes every month, even though the interest rate doesn't.

MOVING EXPENSES

Moving can be expensive, so it's a good idea to create a mini-budget to avoid getting caught off guard by unexpected costs. Whether you choose to hire movers or tackle the move yourself, make sure you're aware of all the potential costs, plus how and when these costs will have to be paid.

IF YOU HIRE A MOVING COMPANY

Before you hire movers, get estimates from a few different companies. Costs can vary widely, so find out exactly what you're getting for the price. Here are the most common items included in moving company estimates:

→ Time and manpower fee

→ Fuel charges

→ Additional insurance (if you have valuable items)

→ Packing materials and services

→ Extra services (such as disconnecting appliances, moving a bunk bed, moving a piano, etc.)

IF YOU'LL BE MOVING YOURSELF

Taking the DIY approach can cost much less than hiring pros, but there are still significant costs to consider:

→ Truck or van base rental fees

→ Gas and mileage charges

→ Insurance (if you pay by credit card, you may already be covered—call the credit card company to find out)

→ Equipment charges (for hand trucks, loading ramps, and furniture covers, for example)

→ Packing materials

MORE POTENTIAL COSTS TO CONSIDER

However you decide to move your belongings, these additional costs might crop up in connection with your move:

→ Storage fees, should you need to store furniture or other items temporarily

→ Cost-of-living differences, because living expenses can be dramatically different in your new neighborhood

→ Parking permits and fees, common when moving to a city

→ Utility hookup charges, when you set up your gas and electric, water/sewer, and cable services

→ Utility deposits, often required if you've never had utility service in your name before

→ Car registration, which may include special excise taxes based on the value of your vehicle

→ Overdraft fees, if you close out your old bank account while there are still checks outstanding or automatic payments pending

SHOULD YOU
Refinance Your Mortgage?
HOW AND WHY

4 QUESTIONS TO HELP YOU DECIDE

These questions can help you decide if refinancing makes good financial sense.

START HERE →

Does your current mortgage have a prepayment penalty?

YES — It can cost thousands of dollars to pay off your mortgage early

NO →

Will the closing costs outweigh the savings? Refinance mortgages come with closing costs that can run around 1–3% of the loan balance.

YES — Pass on refinancing

NO →

Has your credit score improved? This can make you eligible for better interest rates.

NO — Work on increasing your credit score before applying

116

Refinancing your mortgage means you get a new loan to pay off and replace your original mortgage. This can lower your interest rate and shrink your monthly payments, but still may not benefit your finances. Before you commit to refinancing your mortgage, figure out if that fits with your overall financial plans.

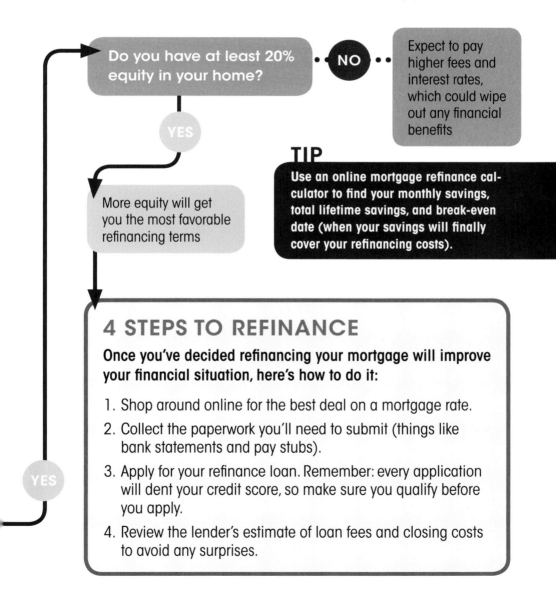

Do you have at least 20% equity in your home?

NO

Expect to pay higher fees and interest rates, which could wipe out any financial benefits

YES

More equity will get you the most favorable refinancing terms

TIP

Use an online mortgage refinance calculator to find your monthly savings, total lifetime savings, and break-even date (when your savings will finally cover your refinancing costs).

4 STEPS TO REFINANCE

Once you've decided refinancing your mortgage will improve your financial situation, here's how to do it:

1. Shop around online for the best deal on a mortgage rate.
2. Collect the paperwork you'll need to submit (things like bank statements and pay stubs).
3. Apply for your refinance loan. Remember: every application will dent your credit score, so make sure you qualify before you apply.
4. Review the lender's estimate of loan fees and closing costs to avoid any surprises.

YES

SELLING YOUR HOUSE

Many homeowners are surprised by how expensive it can be to sell their house. Knowing what to expect can help you set the best price and figure out if you'll be walking away from the sale with any extra cash.

Expect These Expenses

Between getting the house ready, making repairs, and closing costs, there are a lot of expenses linked to selling a house.

PREP AND STAGING COSTS: Spending a little money on things like fresh paint, deep cleaning, landscaping, and minor repairs can translate into thousands of dollars added to the sale price. Staging—making your house look like a model—can also attract buyers.

AVOID SELLING IN THE WINTER—IT'S THE SLOWEST PERIOD FOR HOME SALES.

HOME INSPECTION AND REPAIR COSTS: When the buyer's home inspection inevitably turns up some problems that need fixing, you have two choices: you can make the repairs yourself or give the buyer a credit against the sale price. It's usually a little cheaper (and sometimes more aggravating) to handle the repairs on your own. Getting your house "pre-inspected" can help you work through what you'll do before there's pressure from a buyer.

CLOSING COSTS: When it's time to make the sale, closing costs seal the deal. These usually come out of the sale proceeds. Closing costs include things like:

- Realtor commissions (usually 5–6% of the sale price)
- Appraisals
- Recording and transfer fees
- Title insurance
- Transfer taxes
- Home warranty for the buyer
- Buyer credits (for things like prorated property taxes)
- Your mortgage payoff (which will be a little more than your mortgage balance)

SETTING THE RIGHT PRICE

The number-one rule of selling your house: don't price it too high. Second rule: don't expect to get as much as you're asking. Work with your realtor to come up with a reasonable price based on comparable sales in your area that also leaves some room for negotiating.

MANAGING HOME REPAIRS AND IMPROVEMENTS

If you own a home, expect to make a lot of repairs and improvements. Many will be minor, some even small enough to tackle on your own, but other fixes or renovations will call for professional help and can be expensive. Here's what you need to know about how to pay for the work.

HOW WILL YOU PAY FOR IT?

Emergency fund or project savings: Using savings to pay contractors is the most economical because you won't be charged any interest or finance charges.

Credit card: If the project will cost less than $2,000 and you feel confident you can pay off the charges within three billing cycles, it can make sense to use a credit card. Even though the interest rate is high, you won't have to pay any loan closing costs or financing fees.

Home equity loan: These loans use your home as collateral, and you can borrow up to your equity (the home value minus your mortgage balance). The loan amount, term, interest rate, and payment are all fixed. This loan comes with closing costs, but interest payments are tax deductible.

HELOC (home equity line of credit): This line of credit (LOC) works like a home credit card: you borrow what you need as you need it up to the credit limit (usually your home equity). The loan amount, term, interest rate, and payment all change based on current conditions. The LOC comes with closing costs, and interest payments are tax deductible.

 Contractor financing: AVOID THIS OPTION. Contractor loans often come with very high interest rates, hidden fees, and buried costs.

WILL HOMEOWNERS INSURANCE COVER IT?

Many major repairs can be covered at least partially by homeowners insurance, but there's a lot these policies don't cover, including normal wear and tear and home improvements. Read your policy and call your agent if you're unsure about coverage. Here are some situations that typically would or wouldn't be covered.

WOULD BE COVERED

- Damage caused by flooding from burst pipes, backed up sewers, or broken water heaters
- Mold removal due to sudden water problems that you handle promptly
- Storm damage

WOULDN'T BE COVERED

- Burst pipes, backed up drains, broken water heaters
- Mold caused by long-term leaks
- Flood damage (unless you specifically have flood insurance)
- Infestations by insects or rodents, and the damage they cause

INDEX

ABOUT THE AUTHOR

Michele Cagan is a CPA, author, and financial mentor. With more than twenty years of experience, she offers unique insights into personal financial planning, from breaking out of debt and minimizing taxes to maximizing income and building wealth. Michele has written numerous articles and books about personal finance, investing, and accounting, including *Investing 101*, *Stock Market 101*, and *Financial Words You Should Know*. In addition to her financial know-how, Michele has a not-so-secret love of painting, Star Wars, and chocolate. She lives in Maryland with her son, dogs, cats, and koi. Get more financial guidance from Michele by visiting MicheleCaganCPA.com.

ABOUT THE DESIGNER

Elisabeth Lariviere is an artist and designer who grew up in New England. She studied art and graphic design at the University of Massachusetts Dartmouth, where she discovered her love for printmaking and creating handmade books. When Elisabeth is not designing or creating, she likes to kayak, hike, and camp around the Pacific Northwest; cook vegan meals for her friends; and fix and ride vintage mopeds. She is currently a designer for The Pokémon Company International and lives in Seattle with her adorable dog, Sid.